GREAT WARRIORS

CONQUISTADORS

VALERIE BODDEN

CREATIVE ☕ EDUCATION

Published by Creative Education
P.O. Box 227, Mankato, Minnesota 56002
Creative Education is an imprint of The Creative Company
www.thecreativecompany.us

Design by Stephanie Blumenthal
Production by Christine Vanderbeek
Art direction by Rita Marshall
Printed in the United States of America

Photographs by Alamy (North Wind Picture Archives, The Print Collector), Dreamstime (Ermess, Richard Lammerts), Getty Images (Hulton Archive, Spanish School, Newell Convers Wyeth), iStockphoto (Dimedrol68, javarman3), Shutterstock (Murat Besler), SuperStock (The Art Archive, Image Asset Management Ltd., Newberry Library, Photri Images, SuperStock)

Library of Congress Cataloging-in-Publication Data
Bodden, Valerie.
Conquistadors / Valerie Bodden.
p. cm. — (Great warriors)
Includes bibliographical references and index.
Summary: A simple introduction to the Spanish warriors known as conquistadors, including their history, lifestyle, weapons, and how they remain a part of today's culture through language and traditions.
ISBN 978-1-60818-467-5
1. America—Discovery and exploration—Spanish—Juvenile literature. 2. Conquerors—America—History—Juvenile literature. 3. Conquerors—Spain—History—Juvenile literature. I. Title.
E141.B64 2013
970.01′6—dc23   2012051834

First Edition
2 4 6 8 9 7 5 3 1

TABLE OF CONTENTS

Sometimes people fight.

They fight for food. They fight for land. Or sometimes they fight for sport. Conquistadors (*con-KEES-tuh-dorz*) were warriors who fought the **native** people of **the Americas** to gain land for Spain.

Conquistadors carried flags to help let others know who they were

In 1492, Christopher Columbus sailed to the Americas. He learned of gold, silver, and other riches there. Then other people from Spain went to the Americas. They wanted to get rich, **claim** land for Spain, and spread **Christianity**.

COLUMBUS WAS FRIENDLY TO THE NATIVES
WHEN HIS SHIP FIRST LANDED.

Soldiers helped conquistadors take over lands. Most of the soldiers had fought in wars for Spain's army. When they were done in the army, they wanted to look for riches with the conquistadors.

People thought they would find gold everywhere

A conquistador's favorite weapon was a thin, sharp sword called a rapier (*RAY-pee-ur*). Conquistadors also used guns. The guns made loud noises that scared the native fighters. Conquistadors fought with **crossbows** and cannons, too.

PICTURES OF CONQUISTADORS SHOW THEM IN HEAVY ARMOR,
BUT THEY PROBABLY DID NOT WEAR IT IN BATTLE.

Native fighters did not have powerful weapons. So conquistadors did not have to wear heavy **armor** in battle. They did wear metal helmets, though.

Conquistadors rode horses, while natives did not

Native armies were often much larger than conquistador armies. But conquistadors used their powerful weapons to win most battles. Then they often took over as rulers of the land.

SPANISH SOLDIERS OFTEN ATTACKED VILLAGES
BEFORE THEY TRIED TO MAKE PEACE.

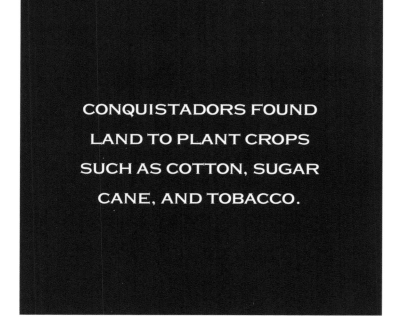

CONQUISTADORS FOUND LAND TO PLANT CROPS SUCH AS COTTON, SUGAR CANE, AND TOBACCO.

Many conquistador soldiers stayed in the Americas. Some of them became farmers. Many married native women and started families.

One of the first conquistadors was Hernán Cortés. In 1519, he fought the Aztecs in Mexico for 80 days. He destroyed their **empire**. Francisco Vásquez de Coronado was another conquistador. He searched for a city made of gold, but he never found it.

Cortés took advantage of the native peoples' kindness

By the late 1500s, many people from Spain had moved to the Americas. For a long time, people from Europe thought the conquistadors were heroes. But they also killed many natives. Conquistadors live on today through the Spanish **culture** and language they brought to the Americas.

MANY NATIVES GOT SICK AND DIED FROM ILLNESSES BROUGHT TO THE AMERICAS.

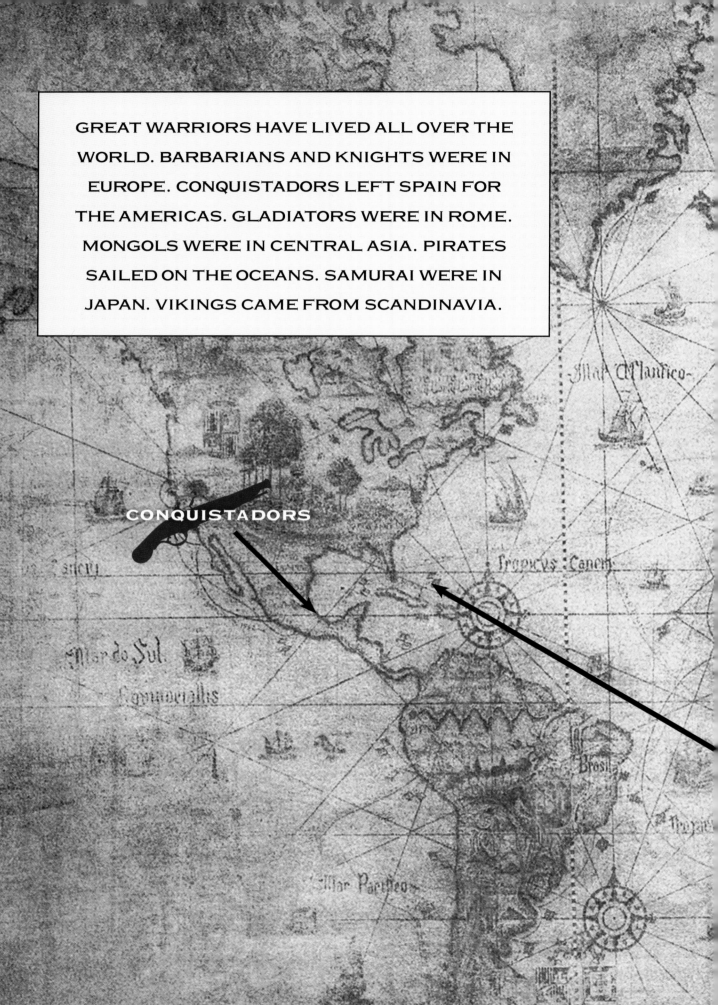

GREAT WARRIORS HAVE LIVED ALL OVER THE WORLD. BARBARIANS AND KNIGHTS WERE IN EUROPE. CONQUISTADORS LEFT SPAIN FOR THE AMERICAS. GLADIATORS WERE IN ROME. MONGOLS WERE IN CENTRAL ASIA. PIRATES SAILED ON THE OCEANS. SAMURAI WERE IN JAPAN. VIKINGS CAME FROM SCANDINAVIA.

CONQUISTADORS

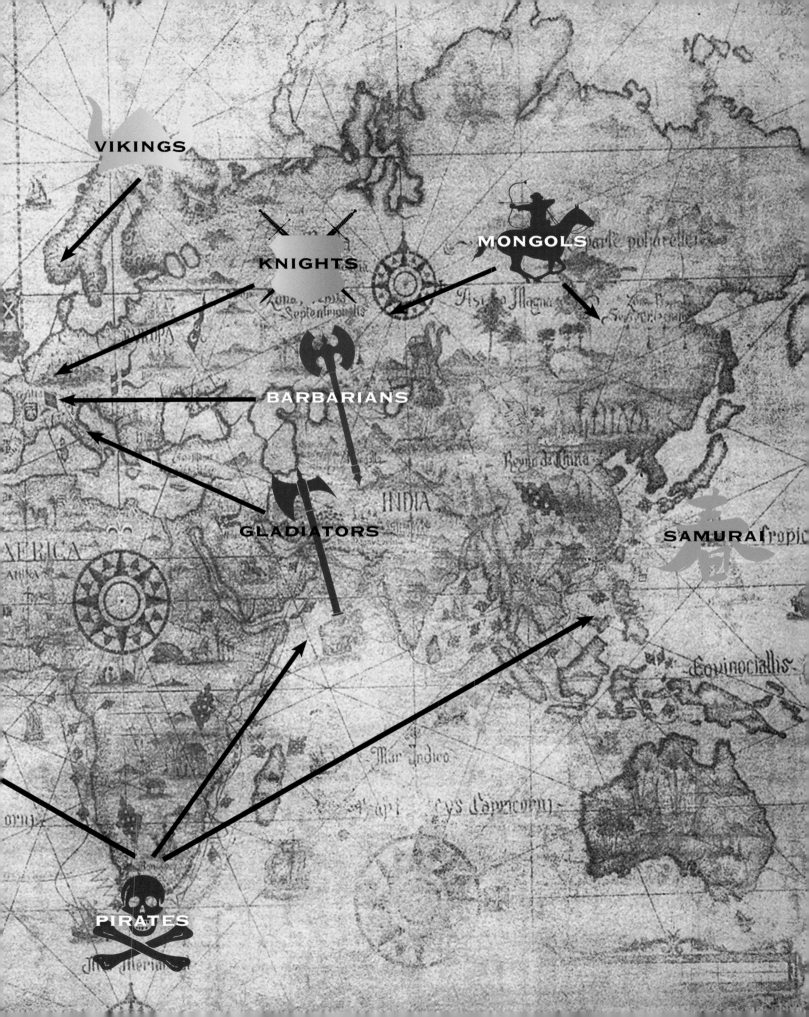

GLOSSARY

the Americas—the part of the world that includes North and South America

armor—metal coverings that conquistadors wore to protect their bodies in battle

Christianity—a religion that teaches that Jesus Christ is the son of God

claim—to say that land belongs to a certain country or person

crossbows—bows that are held sideways and that shoot short, heavy arrows

culture—the ideas, skills, and traditions of a certain group of people

empire—many lands that are ruled by one leader

native—people who are the first to live in a certain place

READ MORE

Ganeri, Anita. *Aztecs and Incas*. Mankato, Minn.: Stargazer, 2010.

Pipe, Jim. *Conquerors & Explorers*. Mankato, Minn.: Stargazer, 2010.

INDEX